TO

_____

FROM

_____

GO THE DISTANCE

AMAZING STORIES OF COURAGE AND INSPIRATION

BY DAN GREEN

GIFT BOOKS
from Hallmark

simple truths®
THE GIFT OF INSPIRATION

INTRODUCTION

Over the last ten years, I've had incredible success in life, sports, and business. But it certainly hasn't always been easy. In fact, it often felt as though it would have been easier to give up—but that's never been my style. By embracing an attitude to never give up and finish strong, I've created a personal level of accountability that goes with me wherever I go. I don't always get the result I want. But during difficult times, I always felt a greater sense of accomplishment and satisfaction knowing that I gave it all I had. When faced with adversity, I remind myself that regardless of what came before or what has yet to come, what matters most right now is how I choose to respond to the challenge before me. **Will I lie down or will I fight? The choice is mine.**

The first time I really discovered the power of this mind-set was early in my selling career. In the early nineties I sold software systems to commercial banks, and a great deal of my selling efforts involved prospecting for leads over the phone. No matter how good you are at selling over the phone, it can be challenging to push yourself to make one more call—and a key to success in selling is "making one more call." As a method of daily goal setting, I started each workday by placing twenty-five paper clips on a coaster next to the phone.

Each time I engaged in a meaningful selling conversation, I moved a paper clip back to the holder. I knew that if I had twenty-five selling conversations each day, I'd reach my ultimate sales goals. I made a commitment not to leave the office until every paper clip was put back. There were many days when everyone else had gone home and I had one paper clip sitting there staring at me. I always dialed until I had one last selling conversation. I never left a paper clip sitting on the coaster and I never put one back that I did not earn. The level of activity I created during this time stuffed my sales pipeline with opportunities. My career took off and I tripled my income in the course of two years—all because I chose to work hard and go the distance.

Because of my sales successes, I had the good fortune to pursue another passion of mine—motorsports. I dreamed of racing at the Indy 500. (I like to dream big.) Living in Indianapolis, I was exposed to the intoxicating world of motorsports. So I went to racing school to learn to drive open-wheel race cars. After a year racing in the Skip Barber Race Series, a racing friend of mine took me under his wing and I ended up signing up to race one of my friend's brother's Formula Fords in the Sports Car Club of America Series (SCCA).

My first race was in October of 1993 at Gateway International in St. Louis, Missouri. As the race started, I hung with the leaders for the first quarter of the race. They were a bit quicker than me, and by the midpoint of the race, they had pulled into a half-lap lead. Frustrated, I began pushing the limits of my car in an effort to catch them. As a result, I pushed my car deep into a corner and lost control, spinning out and losing valuable time. Though I was able to get back on track quickly, it seemed unlikely that I would catch the leaders.

My mistake was devastating and winning seemed out of reach. Sitting in the cockpit, speeding down the backstretch with the cars behind quickly catching up, I had a decision to make. Should I get down on myself and coast around the final laps in despair? Or should I pull my belts tight, put my nose down, and set a new, realistic goal? I drew upon my commitment to rise to the challenge and decided to try to turn the fastest lap of the race. I remember saying out loud, "Come on, Dan, finish strong!" I controlled my emotions and got going. My vision cleared, everything slowed down around me, and my focus intensified.

On the next-to-last lap, I passed two cars ahead of me. Coming out of the last turn with one lap to go, I could barely see the two leaders at the end of the front stretch diving into turn one. As I came through the turn, I was shocked to see that the number one and two cars ahead of me had crashed and taken themselves out of the race. I couldn't believe it. Coming out of the last turn, I saw the checkered flag waving. I won! I was shocked. If I'd given up after my spin I never would've caught and passed the two cars in front of me and put myself in a position to win. By choosing to press on I ended up winning the first SCCA race I entered. In racing, they say that in order to finish first you must first finish. True, but finishing strong is even better.

The purpose of this book is to introduce you to this attitude and the power of positive thinking. I hope that you will embrace it. The stories I've chosen are amazing examples of people who exemplify this spirit in sports and in life. My wish for you is to always follow your dreams and go the distance, no matter what obstacles you face.

Dan

JOHN BAKER
RUNNER AND TRACK COACH

Everyone said John Baker was too short and slight to be a runner for his high school track team. But John loved to run, and he wanted to make the team. His best friend, John Haaland, was a tall and promising runner who was heavily recruited by the Manzano High School track coach, but he wanted nothing to do with the sport. Under the premise that his best friend would follow, John Baker convinced the track coach to let him join the team. The coach agreed and John Baker became a runner.

The team's first meet was a 1.7-mile cross-country race through the foothills of Albuquerque. The reigning state champion, Lloyd Goff, was running and all eyes were on him. The race began and the pack of runners led by Goff disappeared behind the hill. The spectators waited. A minute passed, then two and three. Finally, the silhouette of a single runner appeared. To everyone's amazement, it was not Goff, but John Baker who led the way to the finish line. In his first meet, he blew away the field and set a new meet record.

When asked what happened behind the hill, Baker explained that during the halfway point of the run, he was struggling. He asked himself a question:

"Am I doing my best?"

Still unsure if he truly was giving his best effort, he fixed his eyes on the back of the runner in front of him.

"One at a time," he thought. His entire focus was on one thing— passing the runner in front of him.

He was determined to let nothing distract him—fatigue, pain, nothing. One by one, he caught and passed each runner in front of him until there was no one else to pass.

As the season progressed, John proved that his first race was not a fluke. Once each race began, the fun-loving, unassuming teenager became a fierce and relentless competitor who refused to lose. By the end of his junior year, John broke six meet records and was largely regarded to be the best miler in the state. In his senior year he ran the entire track and cross-country season undefeated, winning the state championship in both events. The future certainly looked bright for the seventeen-year-old.

John entered the University of New Mexico in 1962 and took his training to the next level, running over ten miles a day. In the spring of 1965, Baker and his team faced the most feared team in track—the University of Southern California Trojans. There was little doubt that the mile belonged to the Trojans. During the race, Baker led for the first lap then purposely slipped back to fourth. At the far turn of the third lap, he collided with another

runner vying for position. Baker stumbled, struggling to stay on his feet and losing valuable time. **With just under 330 yards to go, Baker dug deep and, living up to his reputation, blew past the leaders to take the victory by three seconds.**

The future looked even brighter for John Baker. After graduating college, Baker set his sights on the 1972 Olympics. In order to have time to train and also make a living, John took a coaching position at Aspen Elementary in Albuquerque where he had the opportunity to work with kids—something he always wanted to do. Within a few months, Coach Baker became known as the coach who cared. He invested a great deal of time and energy into working with his students as individuals. He was not a critical coach, but only demanded what he demanded of himself—that each child

give his best effort. The kids responded and loved learning from Coach Baker.

In May 1969, just before his twenty-fifth birthday, John noticed that he was tiring prematurely from his workouts. Soon after, he developed chest pains and woke with a painfully swollen groin. He went to see his doctor, who discovered that John had an advanced form of testicular cancer. The only chance John had was to undergo surgery. The operation confirmed the worst: John's cancer had spread. His doctor believed that, at best, he had six months to live. A second operation was required.

The devastation that John Baker must have felt is unimaginable. How easy it would have been to lie down, quit, and feel sorry for himself. In fact, shortly before the second operation, John drove to the mountains and prepared to end his life, for he didn't want to put his family through the pain. Just before he thought of driving off the cliff, he recalled the faces of the kids at Aspen Elementary and wondered if they would think that this was the best Coach Baker could do. This was not the legacy he wanted to leave behind.

At that moment, he decided to rededicate his life to his kids and continue striving to give his best effort. John was not a quitter. He drove home determined to live his life to the fullest.

In September, after extensive surgery and a summer of treatments, John returned to Aspen where he added a unique program to include handicapped kids within the sports program. He appointed kids as "Coach's Timekeeper" or "Chief Equipment Supervisor." Everyone was included. By Thanksgiving, letters from parents arrived daily at Aspen Elementary in praise of Coach Baker. John created a special award for any child that he thought deserved recognition. He used his own trophies as awards, carefully polishing off his name. He purchased special fabric with his own money and cut blue ribbons to give as awards.

John refused to take medication to help with his pain because he was afraid of how it might impair his ability to work with the kids. In early 1970, John was asked to help coach a small Albuquerque track club for girls—The Duke City Dashers. By that summer, the Dashers were a team to contend with. Baker boldly predicted that they would make it to the AAU finals.

By now, Baker's condition was complicated by the chemotherapy treatments. He could not keep any food down, his health rapidly deteriorated, and he struggled to make it to practices. At one October practice, a girl ran up to Coach Baker and shouted, "Coach, your prediction came true! We're going to the AAU championship next month." Baker was elated and hoped for one remaining wish to come true—to live long enough to go along. Unfortunately, it was not to be. A few weeks later, John clutched his abdomen and collapsed. He was not able to make the trip. At the age of twenty-six, on Thanksgiving Day in 1970, John Baker passed away—eighteen months after his first visit to the doctor. He beat the odds by twelve months. Two days later, the Duke City Dashers won the AAU championship in St. Louis—for Coach Baker.

A few days after his funeral, the children at Aspen Elementary began calling their school "John Baker School," and others rapidly adopted the change. A call to make the new name official began. The Aspen principal referred the matter to the Albuquerque school board. In the spring of 1971, 520 families in the Aspen district voted on the matter. There were 520 votes for the name change and none against. That May, at a ceremony attended by hundreds of Baker's friends, family, and kids, Aspen Elementary officially became John Baker Elementary.

Today John Baker Elementary stands as a testament to a courageous young man who believed in giving his best effort right down to the very end. His legacy continues through the dedicated efforts of the John Baker Foundation. The following poem is used with the permission of his foundation and was written by John five years before he was diagnosed with cancer:

Many thoughts race through my mind
As I step up to the starting line
Butterflies thru my stomach fly
And as I free that last deep sigh,
I feel that death is drawing near,
But the end of the race I do not fear.
For when the string comes across my breast,
I know it's time for eternal rest.

The gun goes off, the race is run,

And only God knows if I've won.

My family and friends and many more

Can't understand what it was for.

But this "Race to Death" is a final test,

And I'm not afraid, for I've done my best.

— JOHN BAKER

BETHANY HAMILTON
PROFESSIONAL SURFER

It was a perfect day for surfing off the coast of Maui. A thirteen-year-old surfing prodigy had just finished riding a twenty-foot wave and was lying facedown on her surfboard. Preparing to paddle out to catch another wave, her thoughts of becoming a professional surfer shifted in an instant. Without warning, she felt a tug on her left arm, and a split second later, she realized that she'd been attacked by a shark.

As she struggled to gain her composure, she realized something even more horrifying–the fourteen-foot tiger shark had bitten clean through her board, taking her left arm in a single bite. At that moment in time, survival, not surfing, became her priority.

Bethany Hamilton learned to surf at the age of four. When she was eight, she entered her first contest and won both of the events that she competed in. At age ten, she placed first in the "11-under girls," first in the "15-under girls," and second in the "12-under boys" division at the Volcom Puffer Fish contest. She was determined to become a professional surfer and was certainly on track to make it happen. Then, in one violently swift moment that fall day in 2003, it seemed her dreams were shattered.

However, Bethany had the heart of a lion and the competitive spirit of a thoroughbred. She was determined to return to the water. Leaning on support from her friends and family and her faith in God, Bethany recovered rapidly and, just ten weeks after the attack, was surfing again. Convinced she could overcome her physical challenge, she worked hard to learn to surf with her disability. But she also had to overcome the psychological fear of another attack. Bethany faced her fears by singing and praying when she was out on the water.

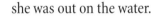

Incredible as it seems, less than a year after the attack, Bethany returned to competition.

She took fifth place at the National Surfing Championships and first place at the first event for the Hawaii National Scholastic Surfing Association. She was recognized by ESPN in 2004 and received an ESPY award for Best Comeback Athlete of the year.

Because Bethany never gave up and overcame her physical and mental challenges, she is in an elite class of achievers. Her unique ability to confront her fears, embrace them, and then continue moving forward in the direction of her goals is the perfect definition of courage.

"Most of us have far more **courage** than we ever dreamed we possessed."

—DALE CARNEGIE

SIR ERNEST SHACKLETON

ANTARCTIC EXPEDITION LEADER

On August 1, 1914, Sir Ernest Shackleton set sail with a crew of twenty-eight on an expedition to the Antarctic. Their goal was to cross the Antarctic on foot—something never done before. Shackleton was a successful and highly respected explorer known for his faith, determination, and conviction. He was knighted for his successful expedition to Antarctica in 1907-09.

To recruit his crew, he took applications from five thousand men. Many believe that he placed the following ad in a London newspaper to attract the applicants.

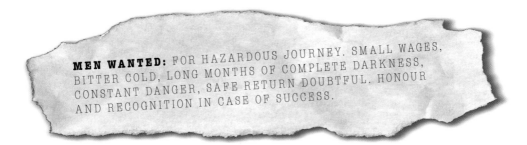

MEN WANTED: FOR HAZARDOUS JOURNEY. SMALL WAGES, BITTER COLD, LONG MONTHS OF COMPLETE DARKNESS, CONSTANT DANGER, SAFE RETURN DOUBTFUL. HONOUR AND RECOGNITION IN CASE OF SUCCESS.

While there is no evidence that this ad actually ran, it does quite appropriately frame the environment for which Shackleton was trying to recruit.

This expedition turned out to be different than any other that Shackleton had led. Five months into the expedition, their ship, the Endurance, got stuck in the heavy ice floes near Antarctica. It was not uncommon for ships to get caught in the ice floe.

Shackleton believed that the ice would eventually recede and free the ship. His focus was on the expedition and he held fast to that course.

However, over the next three weeks the ship became solidly frozen in the ice. Attempts to free the ship were futile. At the end of February 1915, the crew prepared the ship to become their camp for the remainder of winter. At this point, Shackleton abandoned his primary goal for the expedition and turned his focus toward returning to England. His expedition had become a survival mission.

After eight months, the pressure created by the ice finally took its toll on the Endurance. The ship began to come apart and sink, making it uninhabitable. The order to abandon ship was given and the entire crew began to salvage as many supplies as they could. They took the sled dogs, food, gear, and three lifeboats and moved their camp to the ice floe next to their sinking ship. The temperatures were brutal, reaching an average of -15°F. For the next five months, the expedition camped on the ice floe surviving on what little food they had left. In April, the ice began to break apart. Shackleton ordered the crew to take only essential supplies and board the lifeboats. They fled the disintegrating ice floe and traveled seven days by sea to Elephant Island. Elephant Island was a barren place to be stranded, made up mostly of snow-covered rock, with temperatures reaching -20°.

For the next nine months, under Shackleton's leadership, the broken expedition remained loyal, optimistic, focused, and faithful to their leader's belief that they would survive. Ultimately, Shackleton knew that their survival depended upon his ability to reach a whaling outpost more than eight hundred miles across the most treacherous ocean seas in the world. Determined to save his crew, Shackleton set out in one of the lifeboats with five crew members. Though the odds of making it were slim, Shackleton successfully journeyed to the outpost and returned to Elephant Island with a rescue party four months later. Nautical scholars consider this journey by lifeboat to be one of the greatest nautical accomplishments in maritime history.

On August 30, 1916, after twenty-two months of being stranded on a barren rock in subzero temperatures, the crew of the Endurance was rescued. All twenty-eight crew members survived the ordeal, and most were quick to credit the strong faith of their leader as the catalyst in their survival.

PAUL HAMM

Going into the 2004 Summer Olympics in Athens, expectations were very high for Paul Hamm. He was the reigning world champion—the first American man to ever win a world all-around title. Though Peter Vidmar medaled in the 1984 Olympics, no American had ever won the men's all-around gold medal in gymnastics, and Paul was expected to change that. If nothing else, he seemed destined to at least join Vidmar by winning some sort of medal.

Hamm started strong in the first three events and held a first place lead in the all-around by .038 points. Then disaster struck. During his vault performance, he under-rotated and missed his landing, forcing him to sit down and nearly fall off the platform.

His score reflected the "cardinal sin" of gymnastics and after the vault competition was over, Hamm found himself in twelfth place. Television viewers around the world saw him sitting on the sidelines with a pale look on his face. It was pretty clear by his reaction he believed he had blown his chance of making history. But this is where Paul Hamm demonstrated the difference between mediocrity and greatness. **He decided to put his fall behind him and move forward, giving his all for the rest of the competition.** He was first up in the next event—the parallel bars. He pulled off a great routine and nailed his dismount. During the next rotation, a few of the competitors in the sixth through eleventh places struggled. His great performance on the parallel bars, coupled with the struggles of his competitors, helped to move Hamm into fourth place in the all-around with his last and strongest event remaining—the high bar.

Paul was determined to take advantage of this positive turn of events and make sure that he at least won the bronze medal. He was a master of the high bar and had scripted a highly technical routine in order to have a shot at earning the most points possible. As the final competitor, the die was cast.

+.012

Paul poured his heart into the routine—his energy, focus, and determination were palpable. When he nailed his dismount, it was electrifying. Even before his score was revealed, Paul's face showed that in his own mind he had already won, regardless of the outcome. He came back from a crushing failure on the vault and proved to himself that he could execute beyond failure. And as it turned out, in one of the most dramatic comebacks of all time he won the gold medal in the men's all-around by 0.012 points, becoming the first American man to ever win the Olympic title. Talk about going the distance!

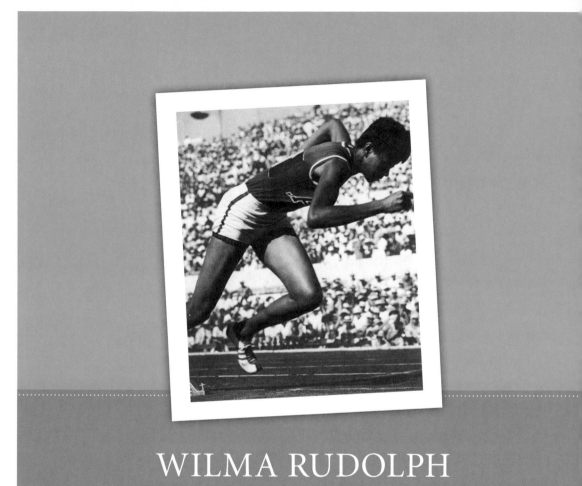

WILMA RUDOLPH

TRACK STAR

On June 23rd, 1940, Wilma Glodean Rudolph, the twentieth of twenty-two children of Ed and Blanche Rudolph, was born prematurely and weighed only 4.5 pounds. The Rudolphs were African-Americans living in a time of segregation. Because the Rudolphs had little money and the local hospital was for whites only, Mrs. Rudolph was forced to care for Wilma herself. Wilma's early years were very rough. She had one illness after another—measles, mumps, scarlet fever, chicken pox, and double pneumonia. A few years after her birth, they discovered that Wilma's left leg and foot were not developing normally and that they were deformed.

The doctors told Mrs. Rudolph that Wilma had polio. They said she would never walk and that she would have to wear steel braces on her legs. Mrs. Rudolph refused to accept this diagnosis and set out to find a cure. She discovered that Wilma could receive treatment at Meharry Hospital in Nashville. For the next two years, Mrs. Rudolph drove Wilma fifty miles each way to get physical therapy. Eventually the hospital staff taught Mrs. Rudolph how to do the physical therapy at home. Everyone in the family worked with Wilma, encouraging her to be strong and get better. Thanks to the patience, support, and love from her family, Wilma walked normally without the assistance of crutches, braces, or corrective shoes by age twelve. She'd spent a great deal of her life limited by her illnesses, and for the first time, she felt freedom. It was then that Wilma decided to become an athlete.

She first pursued basketball, just as her older sister did. For three years, she rode the bench—not playing a single game. But Wilma's spirit was forged from steel and she continued to practice hard, refusing to give up. In her sophomore year, she became the starting guard for the team and led them to a State Championship. But Wilma's first love was running.

It was at the state basketball tournament that Wilma was spotted by Ed Temple, the women's track coach at Tennessee State University. Ed recruited Wilma on a track scholarship and changed the course of her athletic pursuit. At the age of sixteen, barely four years free of braces, Wilma ran the 4x100m relay at the 1956 Olympics. She won a bronze medal.

Wilma's most famous athletic achievement, however, was realized at the 1960 Rome Olympics. **The little girl who couldn't walk without the assistance of crutches or braces overcame her challenges and became the first American woman to win three gold medals in a single Olympics.** Later Wilma became a teacher, inspiring thousands of children with her impressive athletic endeavors and her passion for championing civil rights causes.

"MY MOTHER TAUGHT ME VERY EARLY TO BELIEVE I COULD ACHIEVE ANY ACCOMPLISHMENT I WANTED TO. THE FIRST WAS TO WALK WITHOUT BRACES."

— WILMA RUDOLPH

YEAR	AGE	EVENT	MEDAL	RESULT
1956	16	4X100M RELAY WOMEN	BRONZE	44.9
1960	20	100M WOMEN	GOLD	11.0
1960	20	200M WOMEN	GOLD	24.0
1960	20	4X100M RELAY WOMEN	GOLD	44.5

BEN HOGAN

PROFESSIONAL GOLFER

Ben Hogan was nine years old when his father committed suicide in front of him. It was a horrible thing for a father to do to a son, and it deeply impacted that little boy. Ben turned to golf to escape the horrors of his childhood. While working as a caddie at a local course in Ft. Worth, Texas, he hit balls after work until dark. Because it required no interaction with anyone, golf was the perfect game for Ben. He loved the game and the way it felt when he perfectly executed a shot. Some days, he hit so many golf balls his hands bled.

At age seventeen, he set his sights on perfecting the game he loved so much and set out on the professional tour. He failed to make it on the tour, though, and was forced to take a full-time job. Even after this initial setback, he continued to practice, believing that he had what it took to be a great golfer.

A few years later, Ben Hogan made another attempt on the tour. In the process, he met his wife-to-be, Valerie. Valerie was an instant inspiration to Hogan, and she traveled with him from tournament to tournament. During these early years, he struggled to make a living. Again he was forced to give up the game for a job with steady pay. Throughout his financial struggle, he continued to practice, and with the encouragement of his wife, he returned to the tour for a third try.

In 1940, eleven years after turning pro, Ben Hogan won his first professional tournament. For the next four years, he had modest success on the PGA Tour. Still, he had an intense focus and concentration on and off the course. His demeanor projected a cold and unfriendly personality. In fact, it was common for him to walk from shot to shot with his head down, staring at his shoelaces. When he did look up, Hogan's steely grey eyes and cold stare instantly intimidated anyone who caught his glance. Ultimately, this look earned him the nickname "The Hawk," along with a reputation for being an ice-cold, fierce competitor.

11 YEARS BEFORE FIRST PROFESSIONAL WIN

In 1944, just as Ben Hogan was beginning to achieve success on the tour, he chose to serve his country and join the U.S. Air Force. During his service, Ben couldn't play much golf. He read news articles about the great success of his fellow competitor, Byron Nelson, and longed to be back on the links. During the years that Ben served in the war, Nelson dominated the PGA Tour. The press anointed him "Mr. Golf" and "Lord Byron." Nelson's record of eleven wins in one year still stands

today and will likely never be broken. Hogan was both frustrated and motivated by Byron's success and notoriety. He returned to golf in 1945, determined to re-establish himself as the dominate player in the game. And he did. For the next three years, Ben dominated the sport by winning thirty-one events, two PGA Championships, and the U.S. Open.

In 1948, Ben and Valerie were taking a break from the tour. Driving back to Texas, they ran into a dense fog that forced them to slow to less than ten miles per hour. In a split second, a bus pulled out to pass a truck and was directly in the path of the Hogans' car. In a selfless act, Ben threw himself in front of Valerie to protect her from the impact. The bus hit them head on, sending the engine into the driver's seat and the steering column into the back seat. Ben would have been killed instantly if he had not tried

to protect Valerie. Because of his unselfish courage, Valerie suffered only minor injuries.

However, the crash was devastating for Ben and left him clinging to life. He fractured his pelvis, collarbone, and left ankle. Blood clots threatened his life and forced the doctors to limit his blood circulation by tying off principal veins in his legs. The doctors said it was unlikely that he would ever walk again, let alone play professional golf. But Ben was a fierce and determined competitor in sports and life. He was determined to overcome the challenges confronting him, and with great perseverance and the support of his wife, Ben recovered. He gained enough strength to return to golf in 1950, just eleven months after the accident.

In his first tournament back, he forced a play-off with Sam Snead—an amazing accomplishment in and of itself. However, Hogan's physical condition caused him to fade in the play-off and ultimately lose to Snead. Even so, this small success proved to Hogan that he could compete. He continued to practice hard. Today Hogan is credited with being the first professional golfer to actually practice. When asked about this, he replied, **"You hear stories about me beating my brains out practicing, but . . . I was enjoying myself. I couldn't wait to get up in the morning so I could hit balls. When I'm hitting the ball where I want, hard and crisply, it's a joy that very few people experience."**

Five months later he won the U.S. Open, reinforcing his belief in himself. After the accident, Ben's legs were never the same. He could barely walk eighteen holes without collapsing. Due to his poor condition, he only played seven tournaments each year. However, for the next three years, Ben Hogan dominated every tournament he entered. During this time, he won thirteen tournaments, including six majors. In 1953, he only entered six tournaments but won five, including three majors. Winning three majors in a single year was a record that stood for almost fifty years (until 2000, when Tiger Woods accomplished the same feat).

Ben Hogan ultimately retired with

sixty-four professional victories and nine major titles–

six of which came after the car crash. He is known today as

the father of the modern golf swing.

and Tiger Woods and Jack Nicklaus consider him to be the

best ball striker the game has ever seen.

64 VICTORIES

One of his greatest contributions to the game
is the concept of

practice.

Before Hogan, the idea of practicing golf did not exist.
His work ethic and commitment to improvement
are the model for today's touring professional.

Ben Hogan overcame a dark childhood memory, early failures, and a debilitating car crash to become one of the legends of the game. He continued to be an ambassador of the game and charitable organizations long after his retirement. Throughout his life, there were many reasons for Ben Hogan to have simply been finished. Instead, he chose to persevere and to continue fighting until the end.

U.S. HOCKEY TEAM

It was 1980 and the U.S. economy was in a recession. Iran had taken Americans hostage, and the Russians had invaded Afghanistan. With the cold war in full force, President Carter threatened to boycott the Summer Olympics in Moscow in protest of Russia's actions in Afghanistan. Across America, the events of the time were driving American pride and morale to an all-time low in history. But a hockey game was about to change all of that.

At the 1980 Winter Olympics at Lake Placid, the USA hockey team was represented by a collection of young college kids, some with professional hockey aspirations. Under the guidance of their coach, Herb Brooks, the young American athletes became a fast, well-conditioned, cohesive team. While some questioned Brooks's coaching methods, Brooks developed a physically and mentally tough young hockey team.

Brooks knew how dangerous his team could be. He also knew that many of their competitors underestimated his team's potential and had mostly written them off as a medal contender. Brooks used this miscalculation to his team's advantage.

In order to make it to the medal round, the U.S. team had to fight hard in each match. In the opening game against Sweden, they scored with twenty-seven seconds remaining to force a 2-2 tie. This was a significant event for the team because the Americans had not beaten the Swedes since 1960. The tie lifted the team's morale and planted that first seed of "belief."

Next, the Americans dominated a strong Czech team by winning 7-3—with seven different Americans scoring. Again, this was a significant event for the young team to take and build upon because the Czechs were largely believed to be a lock for the silver medal. Team USA won their next three games, ultimately positioning them for the first medal round against the Russians. Belief had turned into passion for the Americans.

No one thought the young U.S. team had a chance at beating the stronger Russian team. The Russians had dominated Olympic hockey for years, and their players were considered to be professionals by all accounts

due to the strength of the European hockey league and the financial backing of the Soviet Union. The Soviets took great pride in their dominance. In fact, just before the start of the Olympics, they crushed the American team 10-3 in an exhibition match at Madison Square Garden. It was a humiliating loss in front of the American fans, and it seemed clear that the Russians were destined for gold.

Fast-forward a few weeks. Team USA finds itself up against the Soviets in the first medal round, battling not only for a medal but for the pride of America. Tensions between Russia and the United States were very high, and this hockey game took on greater meaning for both nations.

The Russians started strong and took a 2-1 lead early in the first period. **With the final seconds winding down in the first period, the Russians made a critical mistake.** Thinking that the period was almost over, they backed off and began skating off the ice. In fact, there was just enough time for USA's Mark Johnson to take a rebounded shot with one second left and drill it into the Russians' net. USA had tied the game 2-2. The Russians scored quickly again in the second period and again the Americans answered, resulting in a 3-3 tie going into the third period. The Russians threw everything they had at the Americans and the young team answered each blow.

Now the Americans no longer hoped that they could beat the Russians; they KNEW they could. Midway through the third period, Mike Eruzione, the team captain, caught the puck and fired it past the Russian goaltender, giving the Americans a 4-3 lead with ten minutes remaining. The field house erupted and the energy level went through the roof. Could they actually pull this off? Ten minutes seemed like an eternity. Team USA needed to fight to hold off the Russian assault. And the Russians fought hard, firing ten shots for every one shot made by the American team. **The level of emotion and energy in the rink was beyond anything you could imagine.**

As the time wound down, the American fans began to chant, "U-S-A! U-S-A!" This was not about a hockey game. It was about American pride. The well-conditioned U.S. team held off the Russians and won. It was truly a "Miracle on Ice."

Today most people believe that this unlikely victory resulted in a gold medal for the U.S. It did not. This win put the team through to the next round, where they later defeated Finland to win the gold. **In six of seven games played, the U.S. team came back from a deficit to win. They truly embodied the spirit of persistence and passion.**

"Do you believe in miracles?"

— AL MICHAELS, *sports broadcaster, made the famous call as time ran out*

MILES LEVIN

TEEN CANCER PATIENT

A fter a two-year battle with cancer, teenager Miles Levin lost his fight. However, during his final years, he found a self-awareness, courage, and wisdom that most of us will never achieve. Miles chose to post his observations on a carepages.com blog, and through his writings, he inspired thousands of people. He wrote with amazing grace and eloquence. Some of his posts were short:

"Dying is not what scares me. It's dying having no impact."

Some were long and philosophical. But each post served a significant purpose in that it challenged the reader to think more deeply about life, death, and making a difference. Through his words, Miles left this world a better place than the one he came into. Here's what Miles said just one month after being diagnosed with terminal cancer:

I went to the driving range the other day and I was thinking...
I was thinking how you start out with a big bucket full of golf balls,
and you just start hitting away carelessly. You have dozens of them,
each individual ball means nothing to you so you just hit, hit, hit.
One ball gone is practically inconsequential when subtracted from
your bottomless bucket. There are no practice swings or technique
re-evaluations after a bad shot, because so many more tries remain.
Yet eventually you start to have to reach down towards the bottom
of the bucket to scavenge for another shot and you realize that tries
are running out. Now with just a handful left, each swing becomes
more meaningful. The right technique becomes more crucial, so
between each shot you take a couple practice swings and a few
deep breaths. There is a very strong need to end on a good note,
even if every preceding shot was terrible, getting it right at the end
means a lot. You know as you tee up your last ball, "This is my final
shot, I want to crush this with perfection; I must make this count."
Limited quantities or limited time brings a new, precious value and
significance to anything you do. Live every day shooting as if it's
your last shot, I know I have to.

— Miles Alpern Levin, July 7, 2005

"I have tried my best to show what it is to **persevere**, and what it means to be **strong**."

— MILES LEVIN

Like Miles suggested, we should treat each day as a precious ball of life. Take your time, take a breath, and take a practice swing. Make each shot—and each day—count!

WILLIAM WILBERFORCE

ABOLITIONIST

Going the distance in life, sports, or business doesn't always involve overcoming a challenge in a single moment in time. When one lives the attitude, it becomes part of life. In some cases, strength comes in the blink of an eye. For example, you may get an extra burst of energy to finish the last repetition in an exercise. However, sometimes it can take a lifetime to realize the benefits of your commitment to reach your goals. A man named William Wilberforce is testimony to this.

Who was William Wilberforce? Besides being a British politician, philanthropist, and abolitionist, he was a man ahead of his time.

Historian and biographer Kevin Belmonte writes that "Harriet Beecher Stowe praised him in the pages of *Uncle Tom's Cabin*. Novelist E. M. Forster compared him to Gandhi. Abraham Lincoln invoked his memory in a celebrated speech. In the houses of parliament, Nelson Mandela recalled his tireless labors on behalf of the sons and daughters of Africa, calling Britain 'the land of William Wilberforce—who dared to stand up to demand that the slaves in our country should be freed.'"

Wilberforce supported the campaign for the complete abolition of slavery and diligently worked toward this goal. In 1787, Wilberforce became the leader of the parliamentary campaign of the Committee for the Abolition of the Slave Trade. In May of 1789, he made his first major speech on the subject of abolition in the House of Commons.

House of Commons

163

NAY

88

YEA

However, getting people to listen was only a small first step. In April of 1791, Wilberforce introduced the first parliamentary bill to abolish the slave trade, which was easily defeated by 163 votes to 88. Six subsequent attempts to pass the bill also failed, the last in 1805. Like any great leader, Wilberforce cast his vision clearly and often, but his desired outcome had not yet come to be. Still, he persisted.

Two years later, the bill came before parliament again with a different result. In March of 1807, the Slave Trade Act was passed, abolishing the slave trade from the British Empire. It was a momentous victory, yet not the ultimate objective that Wilberforce sought. He continued his campaign for the emancipation of all slaves. Finally, on July 26, 1833—over forty-five years after setting out—Wilberforce received news that the bill for the abolition of slavery had passed its third reading in the House of Commons.

Wilberforce died three days later, but the momentum he created saw his vision through. One month after his death, parliament passed the Slavery Abolition Act, giving all slaves in the British Empire their freedom.

"Have the dogged determination to follow through to achieve your goal: Regardless of circumstances or whatever other people say, think, or do."

— PAUL J. MEYER

JULIE MOSS

TRIATHLETE

ABC Sports called it one of the most defining moments in sports. After leading the 1982 Kona, Hawaii Triathlon for more than seven hours, Julie Moss collapsed fifty feet from the finish line. Millions of television viewers watched as Julie staggered and fell, again and again, before finally crawling across the finish line. What they did not see was the mental transformation that took place within Julie during that time. This was a defining moment in her life.

Julie, a twenty-three year-old exercise physiology student, participated in her first triathlon partly to research her thesis. She entered the event because she believed it would provide her with valuable experience to incorporate into her thesis. She didn't consider herself to be an exceptional athlete. "I used to dread getting called onto the court for volleyball or having to serve in tennis," she says of her high school sporting days. "I really wasn't ready for the pressure of leading the race." But leading an Ironman race can have a powerful effect on people, and Julie experienced that firsthand.

During the midpoint of the run portion—the final leg— her desire to simply finish began to evolve into a desire to finish fast and finish first.

50 YARDS

Never in her entire life had she experienced that competitive side of her psyche. However, she was about to experience the effects of poor diet and hydration during the race.

At that time, very little was understood about nutrition, hydration, and high performance activity. The Power Bar hadn't been invented and most athletes believed that bananas and water were the nutritional staples of high performance—we know differently today. With about seven miles to go, Julie's poor diet and lack of hydration caught up with her and she was forced to add intervals of walking. Her body was shutting down, but her mind was not. "It took all my focus just to keep my body working," she recalled. "The image was that I was pretty out of it, but it was taking all my focus just to keep going. I had to concentrate so much on how I placed my foot on the ground. If I was off by a bit, my leg would just buckle."

With one hundred yards to go, Julie's mind began to play tricks on her. She imagined herself running across the finish line and kept trying to run instead of walk to the finish. Later she said that she probably would have won the race if she simply decided to walk instead of run. For the last fifty yards, she continued to fall, rise, step, and fall over again

TO FINISH

and again. Julie was on her hands and knees just feet from the finish line when the second-place runner passed Julie to win the race. A few seconds later, Julie crawled across the finish line in one of the most dramatic finishes in sports history. For Julie, it was much more than a defining moment in sports; it was a defining moment in her life.

Everyone has a defining moment. Julie's just happened to be captured on film and in front of millions of people. She tapped an inner strength that she never knew she possessed and rose above physical and mental adversity in order to achieve her goal. For Julie, this moment in time shifted the course of her life by redefining her physical and mental personal limits.

JIM BRADDOCK

Boxer Jim J. Braddock, the "Cinderella Man," has an amazing story. His is the story of a working man's rise to the top, his fall to the bottom, and his ascension to heights he never imagined he could reach. And because of it all, he discovered the true meaning of life.

Jim Braddock spent the better part of the 1920s boxing in the light heavyweight division. **He had a reputation for being a fierce competitor with a right-hand punch that could stop a bulldozer** His rise through the professional ranks began in 1926. He won most of his fights and earned a respectable reputation and living. By all accounts, Jim Braddock was a successful man with a good life.

Jim's first big shot came on a warm summer night in 1929. He faced Tommy Loughran for the light heavyweight championship of the world. Loughran was a young, bright fighter who knew how dangerous Braddock's right hand could be. He studied Braddock's style and went into the fight with a strategy to avoid the right hand. His research paid off because Braddock was never able to land a solid punch with his right. The fight went fifteen rounds and Braddock lost to Loughran. Braddock took the loss very hard.

Everything Braddock worked to achieve seemed to be gone. But little did he know how much harder things would get. Less than two months after the loss to Loughran, the stock market crashed and thrust America into the Great Depression.

6-22
AFTER LOUGHRAN LOSS

Like millions of Americans, Jim Braddock lost everything with the crash. With no work available, Jim continued to box in order to provide for his family. Unfortunately, Jim's boxing career had hit the skids. He lost sixteen of twenty-two fights. To make matters worse, he shattered his powerful right hand and lost his greatest boxing asset. Under pressure to support his family, Jim quit boxing and filed for government relief. For the next few years, Jim struggled to make ends meet. He worked odd jobs on the docks and took whatever work he could find. His family finances were shaky at best, and at times they had very little food or heat for their apartment. It was during these years that Jim Braddock discovered how important his family was to him. Because of this emotional time in his life, Jim rediscovered the true meaning of winning.

They say that God's timing is never early and never late. No one found this more true than Jim Braddock in 1934. Due to a last-minute cancellation and the dogged determination of his manager, Jim had the opportunity to fight on the undercard for the heavyweight championship bout between Max Baer and Primo Carnera at Madison Square Garden. However, there were compelling reasons for him not to take the fight. For one, the fight was at the heavyweight class and Braddock was not a heavyweight fighter. In fact, he was almost forty pounds lighter than the average heavyweight. Also, his right hand was not the same as before and he was uncertain if it would hold up under the stress. And finally, he had not been training for the fight. None of this mattered to Jim. To him, this was an opportunity to make some money to improve his family's well-being.

As slight a chance as it was, Jim believed he could win, and that meant a better future for his family. Winning now meant so much more than it did before. Audiences were shocked when, with no training and a bum right hand, Braddock knocked out John Griffin in the third round. Jim might not have been so surprised, however. He later said that his time spent working on the docks kept him in shape and also helped him develop a strong left hook—which no one expected.

As word spread of the upset, Braddock's popularity grew, and the fight promoters leveraged this popularity to their advantage. As a result, Braddock was given a shot at John Henry Lewis, a fighter who'd previously beaten Jim. For this fight, Jim was a huge underdog. Yet again, Jim delivered with a tenth-round victory. Jim Braddock became an inspiration to the nation during a time when everyone desperately needed something to cheer about. Millions of Americans related to Jim and his working man's story.

In the spring of 1935, Braddock was matched up against Art Lasky. Lasky was the number-one contender to fight Max Baer, the reigning heavyweight champion. At the time, there were no discussions about Braddock getting a shot at Baer because nobody believed he could beat Lasky. The fight promoters viewed this fight mostly as a way to capitalize on Braddock's popularity and to make a buck off him. No one even considered that Braddock might win. Jim took Lasky to fifteen rounds. He punished Lasky so much that Braddock won a unanimous decision. With this victory, he became the number-one contender to fight Max Baer for the heavyweight championship of the world—less than a year after working on the docks. The Cinderella Man was born.

Braddock faced Max Baer on June 13, 1935, at Madison Square Garden. He entered the ring a 10-1 underdog and gave up over twenty pounds in weight to Baer. Baer was a ferocious fighter with a hammering right hand who had previously killed two other fighters in the ring. Braddock learned a valuable lesson from his earlier loss to Tommy Loughran. He studied Baer's fight footage and strategized to avoid Baer's crushing right hand—just as Loughran had done to him.

In one of the greatest upsets in all sports history, the Cinderella Man battled Baer for fifteen rounds, winning a unanimous decision to become the heavyweight champion of the world.

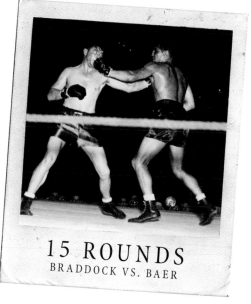

15 ROUNDS
BRADDOCK VS. BAER

In less than a year, Jim Braddock turned his life around completely. Through his personal trials, he was able to redefine the meaning of his life and thus tap into a greater inner strength he never knew he had. This new strength empowered him to achieve his goals. When given the opportunity to make a comeback, his mental shift better prepared him for the fight than any physical training could have done. Jim's new outlook lived on past his boxing career, and he went on to lead a successful and prosperous life until his death in 1974.

KYLE MAYNARD

WRESTLER

Kyle Maynard is a regular guy who loves to compete. He knows that to truly live you must set your sights on a goal and never give up. The fire that burns in his belly helped propel him to contend for the Georgia state high school wrestling championship in 2004. Not such a big deal, you might say—except for the remarkable fact that Kyle has no arms or legs. He was born a congenital amputee—his arms end at his elbows, his legs at his knees.

When Kyle was featured on ESPN in 2004—he won an ESPY award for best athlete with a disability—one immediately noticed how normal he seemed. Kyle did all of the things that any other person or athlete would do. He spoke with passion and conviction, and he never implied that the world owed him anything. Kyle trained hard and lifted weights—he has cannonballs for shoulders. Using a specially designed attachment, he pushed more than double his own body weight. He was surely an inspiration to anyone watching ESPN that day.

From the beginning, Kyle's parents, Anita and Scott, were determined to raise a normal child. They insisted that he learn to feed himself and play with the other kids like any other child would do. When Kyle saw other kids picking up crayons with their fingers, he learned to pick them up using the crease in his short but sensitive biceps.

Kyle's grandmother, Betty, was a source of inspiration as well. She often took him to the grocery store, where she instilled in him a sense of confidence by encouraging Kyle to sit up, smile, and look folks in the eye. He was fitted with prosthetic devices at a young age, but quickly dismissed them because they were too restrictive. He wanted to be free to run and play just like the other kids, and those devices kept him from doing so.

Kyle led an active childhood. He played street hockey with his friends (he was the goalie) and made the sixth-grade football team. Kyle hung tough on the football team, but his physical differences put him at a disadvantage against other players. Eventually his father encouraged him to try another sport that would pit Kyle on an even plane with his competition—wrestling.

When Kyle began wrestling in sixth grade, he lost his first thirty-five matches. It was difficult, but Kyle dug deep and found the confidence to continue. He was a warrior and didn't like to lose. With the support of his father, a former wrestler, Kyle learned to train with weights, built his strength, and learned some moves unique to his capabilities. Kyle overcame the self-doubt he felt during his early wrestling days and became a winner. During his senior year, Kyle won thirty-five times on the varsity squad and qualified for the state championship. In the state tournament, Kyle won his first three matches and even faced his final opponent with a broken nose. Although Kyle didn't win the state championship, he gained confidence and became a source of inspiration for everyone that he met.

Kyle graduated high school and attended the University of Georgia, where he continued to wrestle and inspire others. As a member of the Washington Speaker's Bureau, Kyle regularly gives motivational talks. But what he has to say has little to do with his perceived physical differences. Rather, he speaks of overcoming fear and doubt and what it takes to compete and win—just as any other champion would do. **To this day, Kyle has never been pinned by an opponent. What a fitting metaphor for his life.**

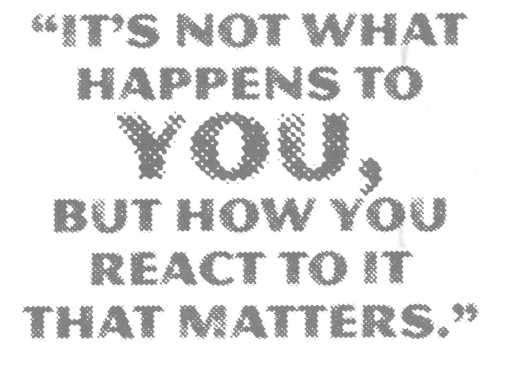

"IT'S NOT WHAT HAPPENS TO YOU, BUT HOW YOU REACT TO IT THAT MATTERS."

— EPICTETUS

HELEN KELLER

AUTHOR AND ACTIVIST

Though her story starkly contrasts many of the athletic endeavors featured in this book, Helen Keller exemplifies the spirit of perseverance and overcoming great adversity to achieve success.

In 1880, Helen was born into an affluent southern family in Alabama. **When she was nineteen months old, Helen was stricken ill and left deaf and blind. Can you imagine the fear that little girl must have felt when her world went dark?** Because of her limited communication, as the years progressed, Helen became demanding, spoiled, and uncontrollable. If it were not for her young friend Martha Washington, the daughter of one of the Keller family's servants, Helen may have been put into a sanitarium to live out her life in complete darkness.

Thankfully, Martha befriended Helen and taught her to communicate with her family through sign language, showing her over sixty signs. Most of us think of Annie Sullivan as the "miracle worker," when in fact it was young Martha that truly helped Helen's world open up. Experts agree that Martha's help was critical to Helen's later success. When Helen was six, her mother reached out to friends to find additional help for Helen. She was referred to a specialist working with deaf children—Alexander Graham Bell. Mr. Bell spent time with Helen and ended up referring her to the Perkins Institute for the Blind. And this is where she met Annie Sullivan.

Annie was a twenty-year-old graduate of the school and was partially blind herself. (She had been completely blind but, through a series of operations, recovered part of her sight.) Annie understood Helen's world. She received permission to take Helen away to help her focus. After secluding Helen and isolating her from her family, Annie was essentially able to break her of her tantrums and ill behavior. Under Annie's guidance, Helen's world opened up exponentially. **Her sight and sound limitations were no longer barriers but, instead, strengths that provided her with great wisdom. She once said, "What I am looking for is not out there, it is in me."**

Helen Keller's achievements have been nothing short of spectacular. She went on to become the first blind person to graduate from college. She traveled the world as a famous speaker and author. Along with numerous other causes, she is remembered as an advocate for people with disabilities. In 1915, she founded Helen Keller International, a nonprofit organization for preventing blindness. In 1920, she helped found the American Civil Liberties Union (ACLU). Keller and Sullivan traveled the world together, meeting international dignitaries from over forty countries. Helen met many amazing people along her journey, including every U.S. president from Grover Cleveland to Lyndon B. Johnson. She befriended many famous figures, including Alexander Graham Bell, Charlie Chaplin, and Mark Twain. Helen passed away in 1968 at the age of eighty-seven.

How could a deaf and blind six-year-old in the 1800s rise to such prominence and make such a difference in the world? Without question, her mother, Martha Washington, and Annie Sullivan deserve a great deal of credit. But the foundation for her success stemmed from within her own spirit. Without the deep-seated desire to learn and to rise above the challenges before her, she could not have overcome her physical limitations, regardless of how much help she had. At the end of the day, we must all eventually look inward to grow outward. Helen understood this better than most. Like many of the people in this book, Helen Keller was a champion who never gave up and truly went the distance.

"We don't see things as they are; we see things as we are."

—ANAIS NIN

TOM OSBORNE

In 1983, the Nebraska Cornhuskers were the team to watch in college football. They opened their season by crushing Penn State, the defending national champions, 44-6. Oklahoma State gave the Cornhuskers their first and only real scare that year. Prior to coming to Stillwater, Nebraska had outscored their opponents 289 to 56 and were the number-one-ranked team in college football, yet they only defeated Oklahoma State 14-10. To further demonstrate what a great team the Cornhuskers were, consider a few of their great players. Mike Rozier won the Heisman Trophy that year. Turner Gill was an absolute wizard to watch at QB. Wide receiver Irving Fryar ultimately became the number-one draft pick in the NFL.

That year Nebraska's head coach was Tom Osborne. He had never won a national championship and was under tremendous pressure to do so. By all accounts, though, he was on his way to leading Nebraska to their first championship. The Cornhuskers had a lot going for them. Osborne's offense was probably the greatest college offense ever to take the field, and the team finished their season with a perfect record. They entered the Orange Bowl as the number-one-ranked team in the country.

They faced the Miami Hurricanes. The Hurricanes entered their season unranked and were slaughtered in their opener by number-seven-ranked Florida. However, that was their first and only loss of the season. The Hurricanes dominated every other game they

played that season. As a result, they were the fourth-ranked team heading into the Orange Bowl. Because of the outcomes of the Cotton Bowl and the Sugar Bowl, the Orange Bowl would be played for the national title. As you can imagine, the game was hyped by the media as the game of the century. **Could the previously unknown Hurricanes actually win? Would Tom Osborne get his first national title? Could the Nebraska offense be stopped?**

The game lived up to the hype. It was an emotional roller coaster to watch and would take too many pages to fully recap. But the simple truth is this: with 1:46 left to play in the game, the Cornhuskers had the ball on Miami's 26-yard line with fourth down and eight to go. They were trailing Miami 31-24. In one of the greatest plays in college football history, Turner Gill ran the option to the right, pitched the ball to Jeff Smith, who ran it in for a touchdown, pulling the Cornhuskers within one point with less than a minute left to play. Nebraska could tie the game with an extra point or win outright with a two-point conversion. Since there was no overtime, a tie game would leave the championship to be decided by the coaches and media polls. But an outright win would seal the championship for the Huskers.

What happened next perfectly defines the meaning of risk. Tom Osborne put the championship on the line and went for two points and the win. He had the best run offense in the country and was completely confident that they could pull it off. He also knew that Miami would be expecting the run. So instead of using his bread-and-butter run offense, he opted to pass the ball. Much to the chagrin of Nebraska fans, Gill's pass fell incomplete and, after a failed onside kick attempt, Nebraska lost their first game of the year. There would be no national championship win for Coach Tom Osborne that year.

The next morning football fans across the country debated the "go-for-two" call. Many argued that given a tie, Nebraska would have easily won the vote for the title. Osborne and his team had a different perspective. They wanted to go the distance and win the game and the championship outright. They took the path that they believed would get them there. **It was a calculated risk that Osborne never second-guessed. In this instance it didn't work, but his team gave it their best shot. To this day, Osborne does not regret his decision.**

"NOBODY WHO EVER GAVE HIS BEST REGRETTED IT!"

— GEORGE HALAS

This is the last chapter in the book, and you've probably noticed a theme throughout. **For most of these champions, their greatness did not end with their greatest accomplishments; rather, they were merely at the beginning of greater things to come.** Each used a moment in time to propel him- or herself forward in life.

Bethany Hamilton survived a shark attack to become a world-class surfer and an inspiration to thousands of people around the world. After achieving his success in boxing, Jim Braddock repaid the government aid money that he was given during his hard times and went on to live a full and prosperous life. John Baker's commitment to give his best effort lives on at the elementary school bearing his name. After her Olympic glory, Wilma Rudolph went on to become a teacher, championing civil rights causes and inspiring thousands of children.

Their positive attitudes are grounded in the principle that you never "get there" in life and that you should always go the distance and continue to move forward. Perhaps one of the best summaries of this concept comes from John Naber, the four-time gold-medal-winning Olympic swimming champion. When asked if winning four Olympic gold medals was the highlight of his life, he replied, "I hope not. I've still got a lot of living left to do, and I hope that my greatest achievement is still in front of me."

May your greatest achievements be in front of you, and may you always go the distance.

"EFFORT ONLY FULLY RELEASES ITS REWARD AFTER A PERSON REFUSES TO QUIT."

— NAPOLEON HILL

DAN GREEN

D an is an entrepreneur with a passion for going the distance in everything he does. Over the past twenty years, he has excelled in a wide variety of endeavors, including his roles as salesman, sales leader, sales trainer, patented inventor, race car driver, author, husband, and father. The personal adoption of a positive, "never-say-die" attitude has been a driving force in Dan's life and a key catalyst for helping him to achieve his goals in business, sports, and life.

Today Dan serves as the Executive Vice President of Simple Truths, where he leads the sales and marketing efforts for the company. He lives outside of Chicago with his wife and their two children. He enjoys spending time with family, playing the guitar, boxing, participating in motorsports, and playing golf.

**If you have enjoyed this book,
we would love to hear from you.**

Please send your comments to:
Hallmark Book Feedback
P.O. Box 419034
Mail Drop 215
Kansas City, MO 64141

Or e-mail us at:
booknotes@hallmark.com

Visit SimpleTruths.com to read more
inspirational stories, or to watch one of our
short inspirational movies.